A girl named Dylan

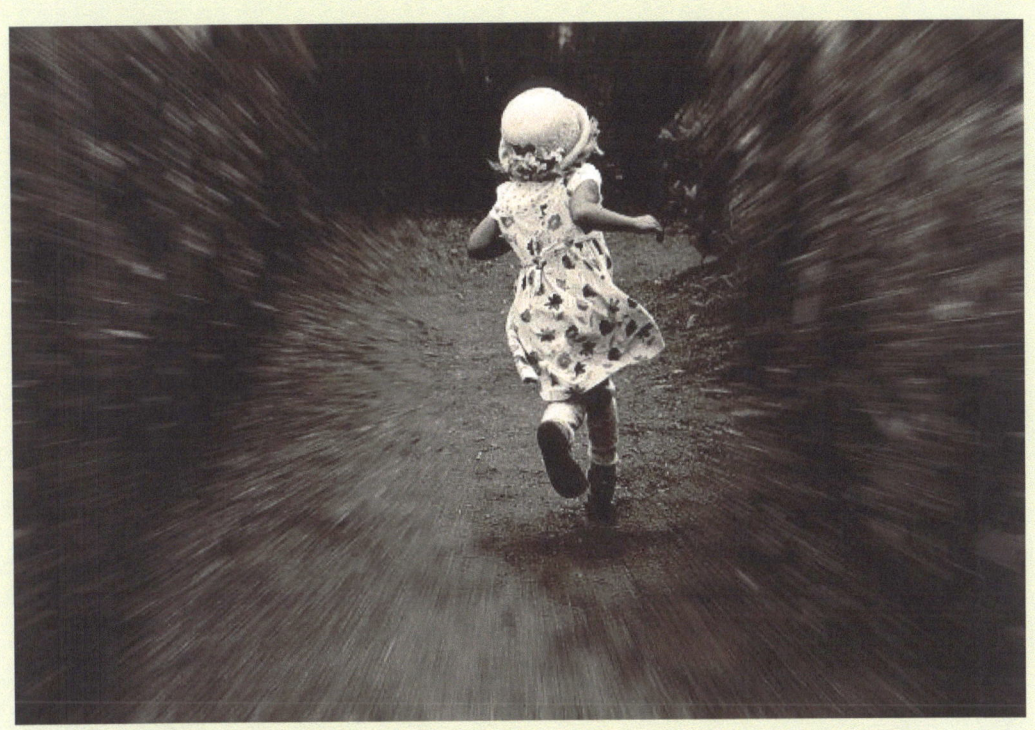

A photographic journey of love

through the eyes of her father

Foreword: Cindy Larson   Images: Brian Daugherty

The Legal Stuff.

All photos are the property of Brian Daugherty.
All rights reserved. Use of photos may be
acquired through permission.
Contact: Brian Daugherty

A girl named Dylan...

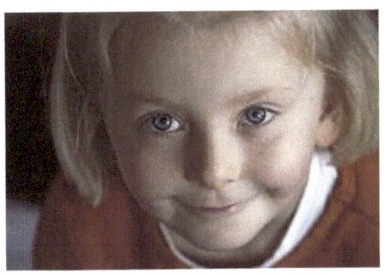

A photographic journey of love

through the eyes of her father

Photography by Brian Daugherty

Thoughts & Quotes by Friends and Family

Created with love by Cindy (his wife)

June 2010

Foreword ~ Dedication

This book is very special as I, and many others, have watched Brian grow as a person through being a father and enjoyed his photography along the way. The laughter and joy Dylan brings to his life is beyond words. His photography does capture glimpses of both the many faces of Dylan and his love for his little girl.

Dylan was born January 27, 2005 on her grandfather's birthday (Brian's dad, Ed). Her birth and life have had a pretty profound effect on her parents who never thought they would be able to have children. Dylan is a gift of pretty phenomenal proportions to us and we realize it. Without a doubt, every day there is truly appreciation for this gift; the gift of Dylan. Dylan's smile, laugh and amazingly funny personality never stop giving. Of course, we like best what her grandmother Carol Ann says, "my beautiful genius."

The intent of publishing his works and sharing with the world is not to make money, but to share an amazing love and happiness through one child's eyes as captured by her father. A portion of the proceeds will go to help children (Rady Children's Hospital - http://www.rchsd.org) and to animal rescue (ASPCA.org) since Dylan and her family love and have for many years rescued animals. Dylan says she wants to be a veterinarian when she grows up. The rest will go to Brian's camera supplies so he can keep taking amazing photos of Dylan and the world.

I hope you enjoy as this journey as much as I have, *Cindy*

Dylan and Tinker 2010, and Wonder Woman and Johnnie 2010

Her rescue dogs

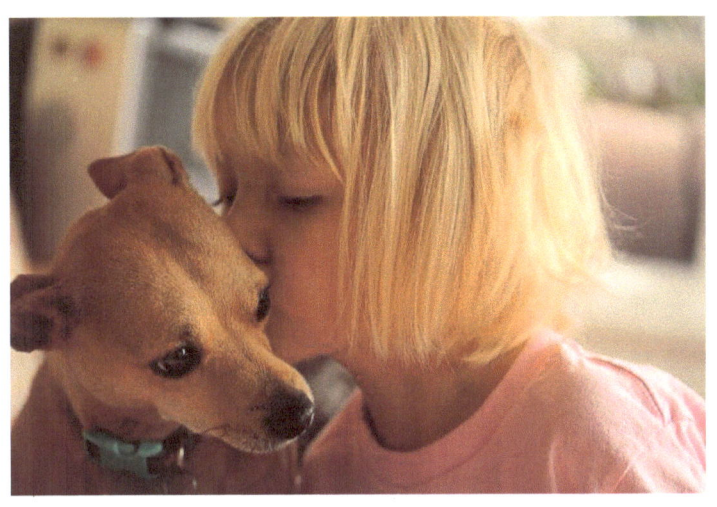

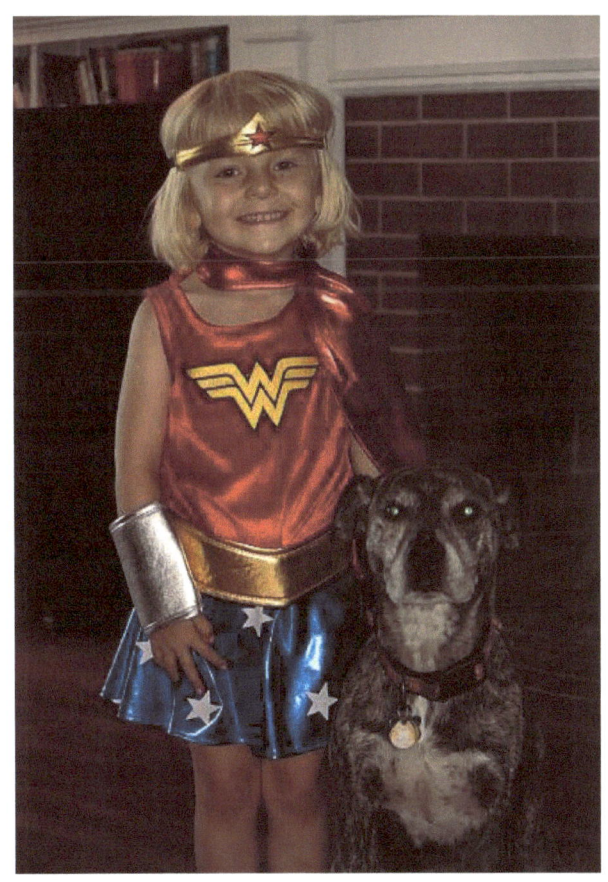

Brian,

Your book came first because as you often say to me, "always have, always will…" be my one true love.. I hope after all these years you know it's mutual.. Thank you.

~ Cindy

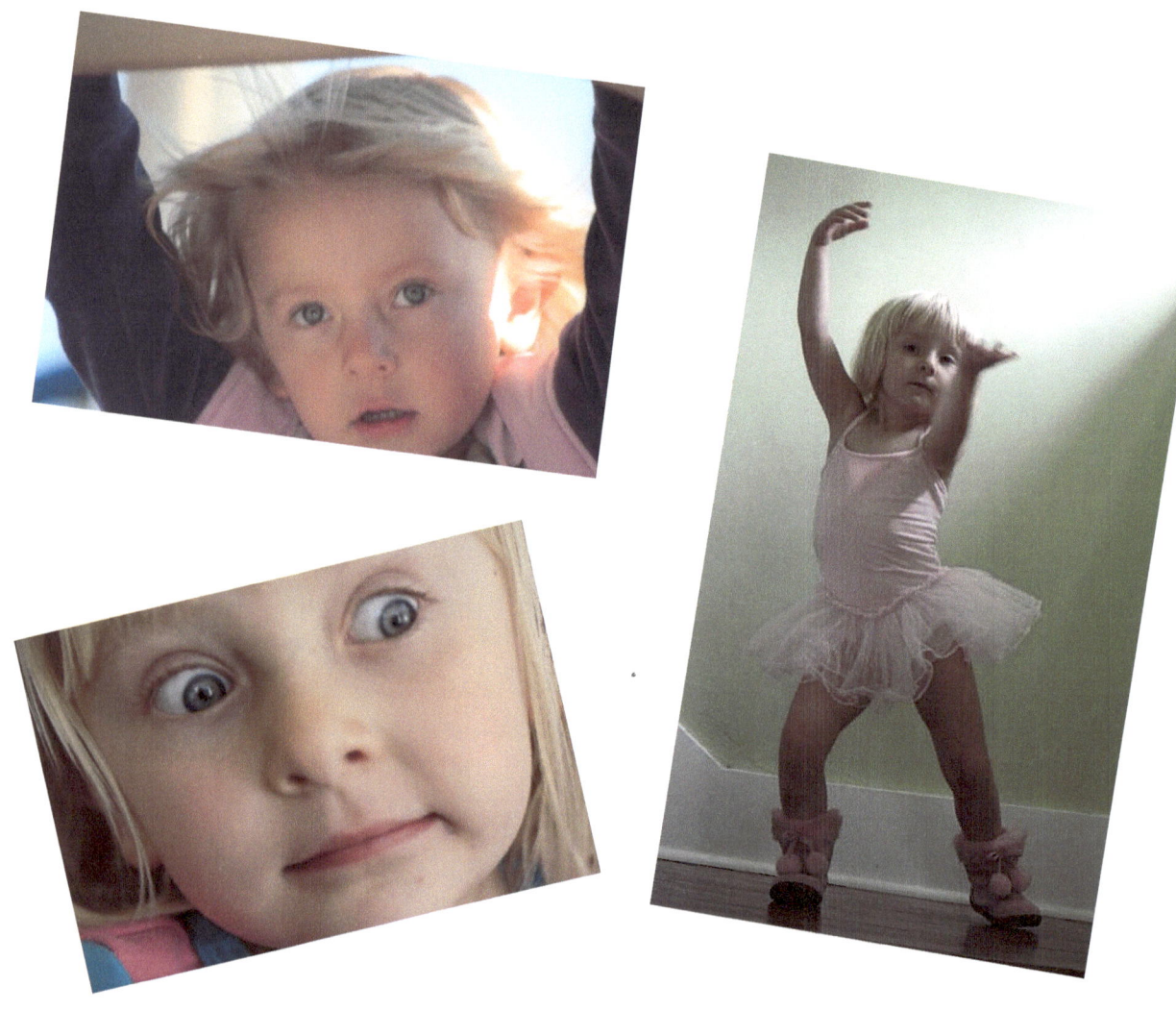

Dylan and Kennedy 2009

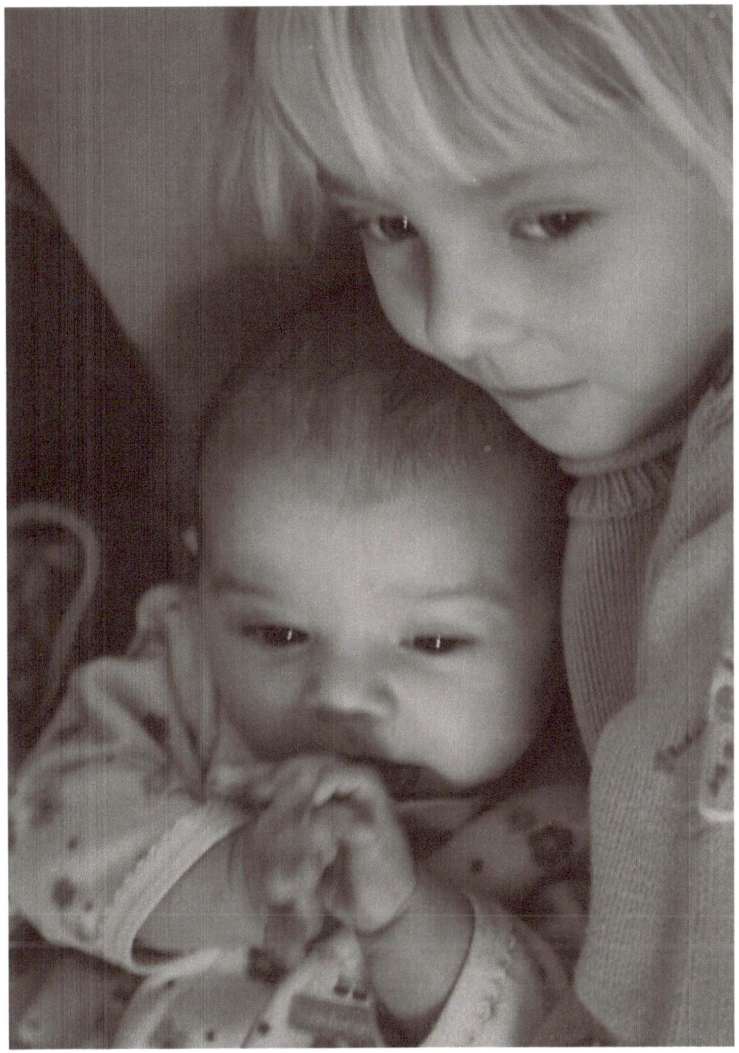

When I think of Brian and his pictures, I think of how it's an expression of his love for others. Brian is very generous with his art and providing access to memories of some of the most important moments of our lives. Brian's heart is in his art and this is how he loves us. I'm thankful for such a generous brother-in-law, father to my niece, husband to my sister, uncle to my son, great uncle to my grand-daughter...he is part of the network that makes up all of us as a family. ....I love you! ~ Carolynn Larson-Garcia

Dylan 2009

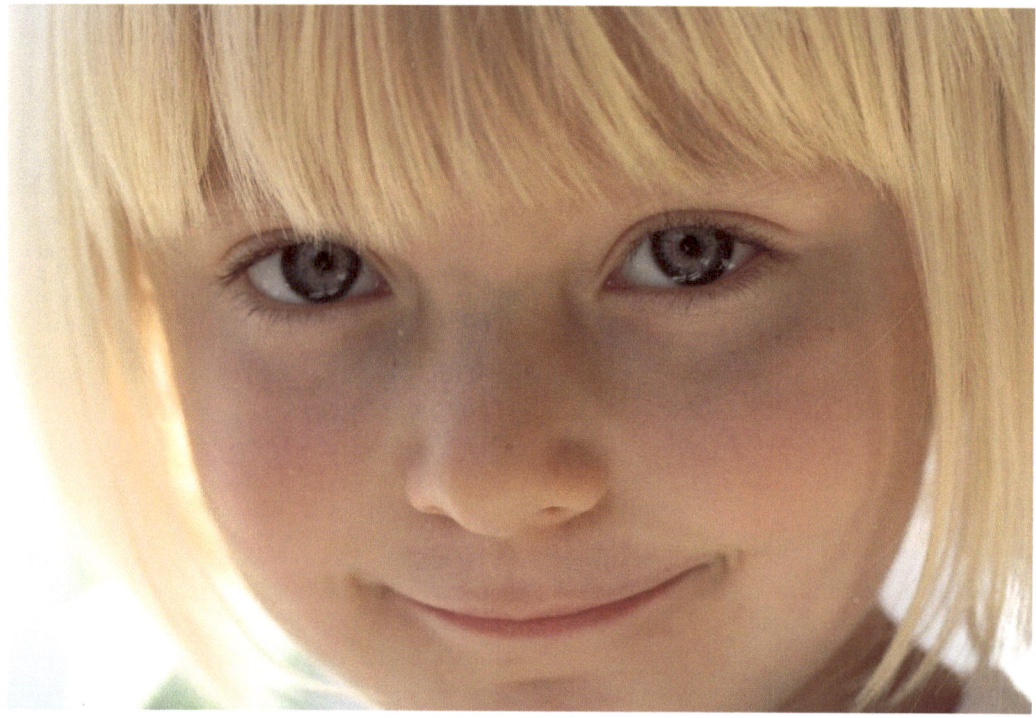

I look into Dylan's eyes in Brian's photos and I see a happy little girl that isn't smiling at the camera, but almost always is smiling at her father who she adores. Brian's pictures remind me how lucky I am to have her and.. him in my life.

~ Cindy Larson-Daugherty

Dylan 2010

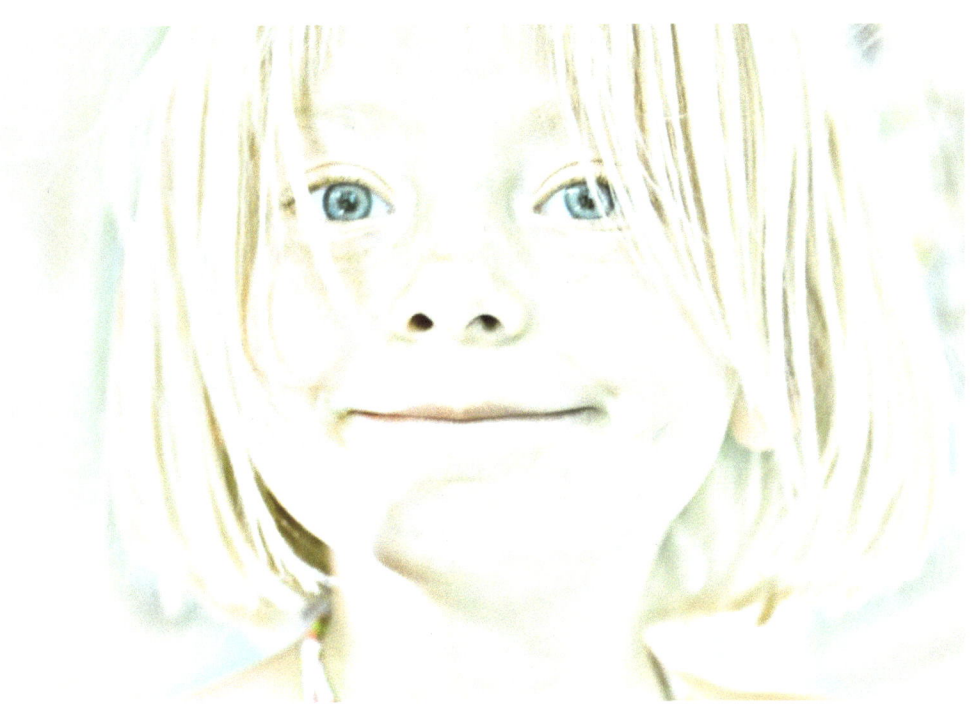

Brian's photos of Dylan remind me of a Louis Kahn quote, "Truly a work of Art is one that tells us, that Nature cannot make what man can make."

~ Ashley Zabel

Dylan 2010

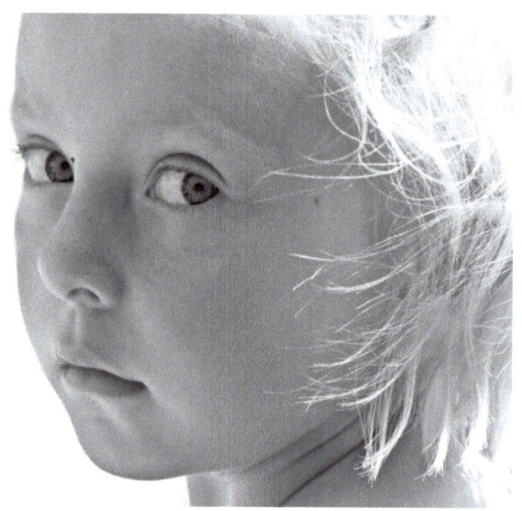

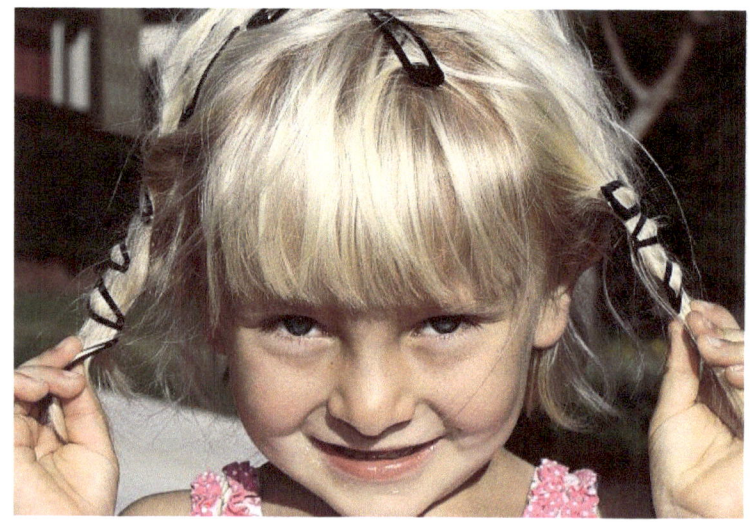

Dylan 2010

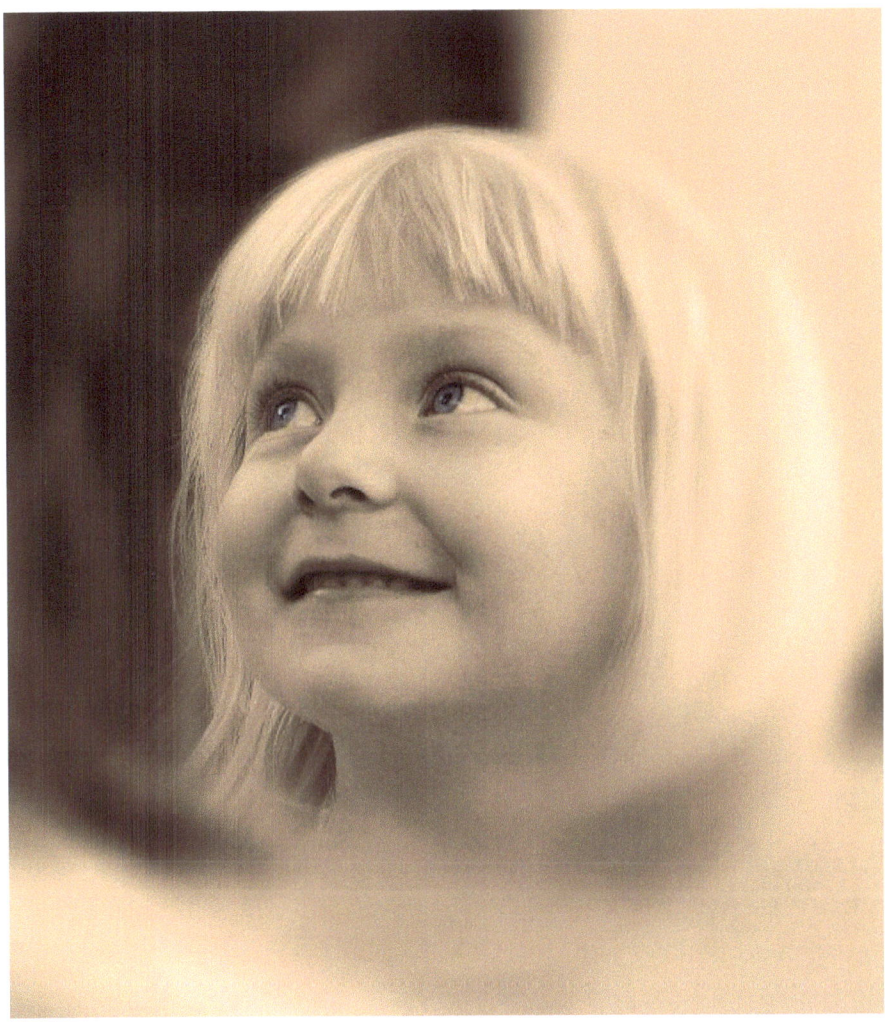

Brian has captured some of our most cherished moments in our life. His ability to create a story through your photos is a family treasure. We love you Brian.

~ Nadene and the Bennett Family

Dylan 2010

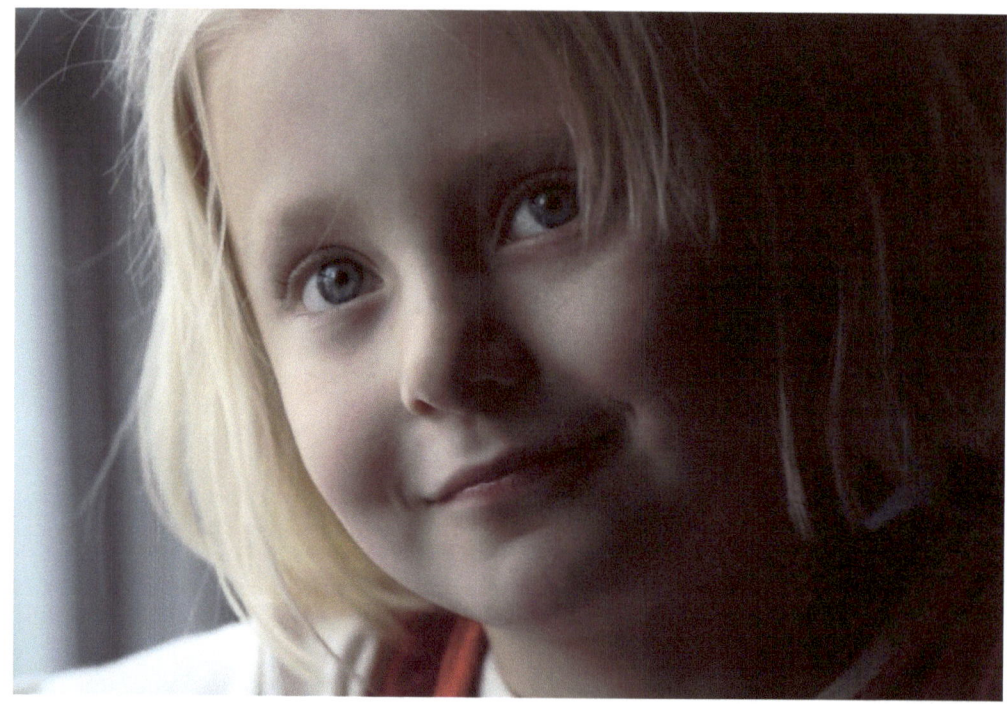

"Brian, and Cindy, are very good at respecting Dylan as a person. They allow her to express herself and have ideas and opinions. They stop and listen when she talks. As a result, she's a good little person and very expressive. Every time I have been around her and them, I see how they interact and bring out her unique qualities. This is just one of many photos that captures her thoughtful, sweet personality. Brian seems to have the ability to capture it almost every time."

~ Kelly Hax

Dylan 2009

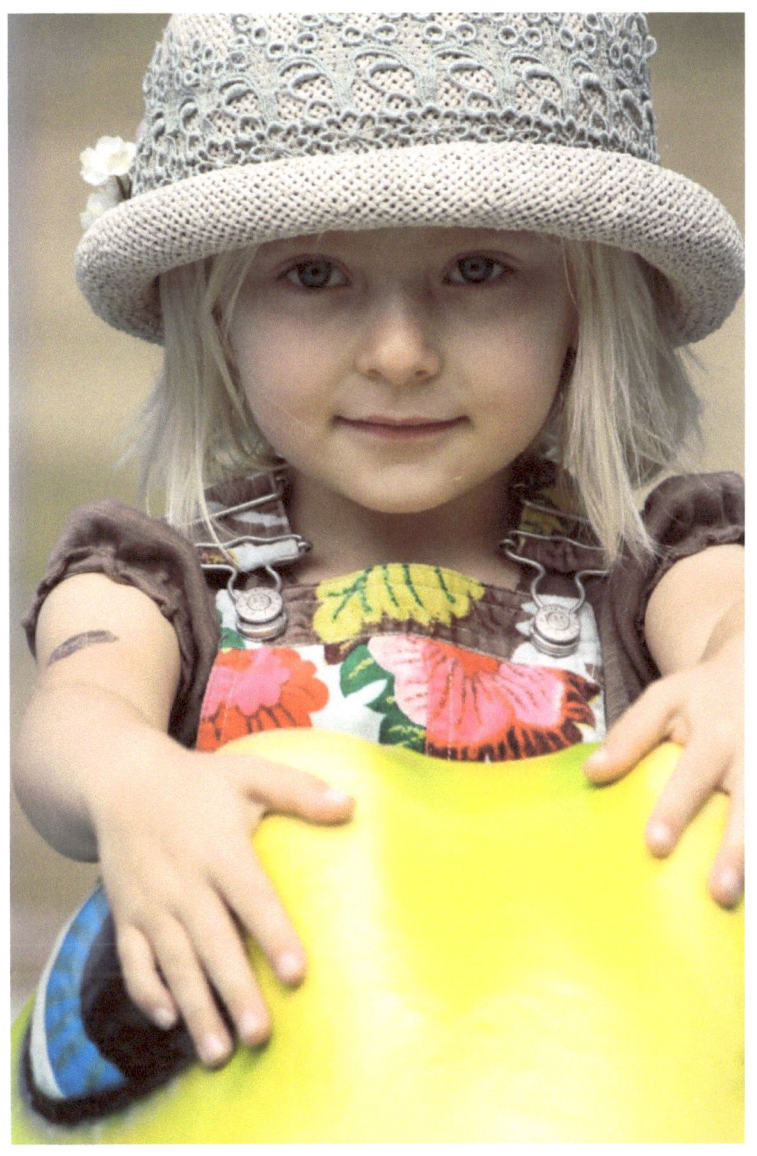

Brian truly lets Dylan just be Dylan. He encourages her to explore and ask questions. He plays, reads, sings, dances, dresses up and dons hair pretties with her. Dylan is a very lucky little lady to have such a loving Dad but I truly believe Brian is aware of how lucky he is too and it shows in all that he does with Dylan. It is beautiful to watch in person and to see in his photos of Dylan and the world.

~ Wendy L. Hershey

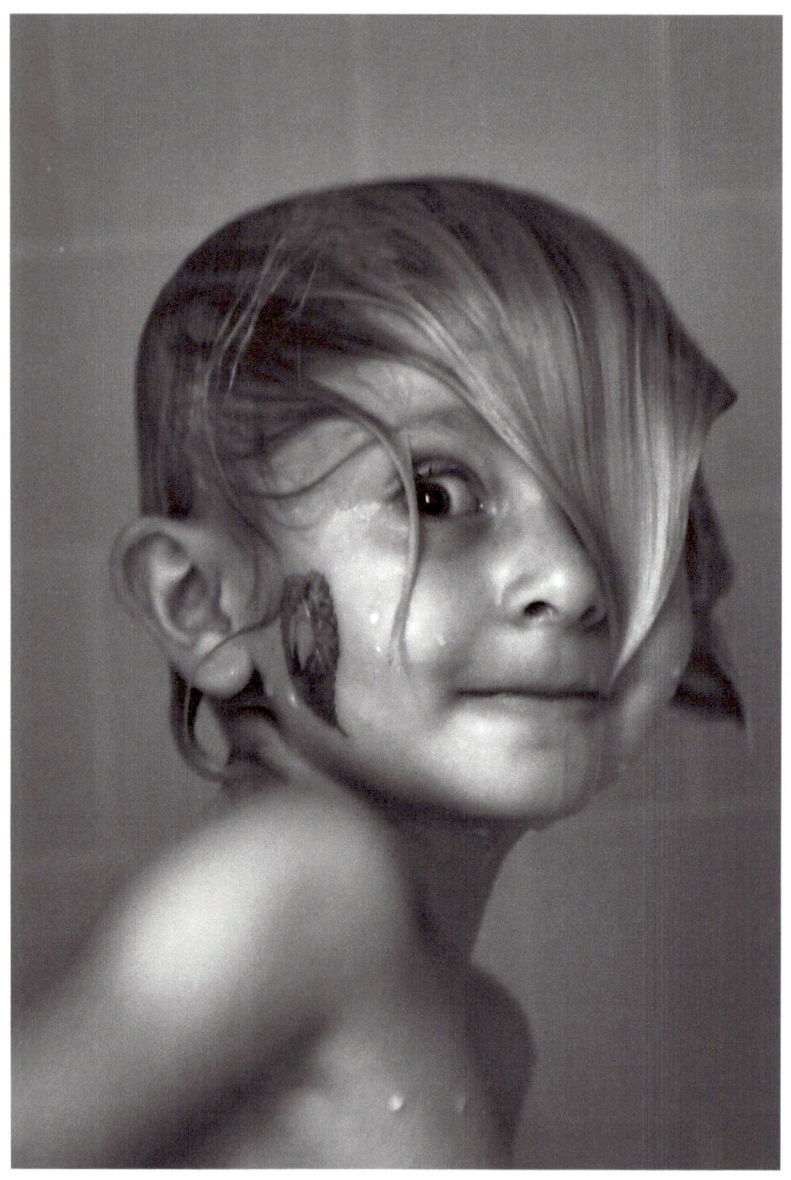

"Adorable Pixie Princess!"

~ Debra Bean

Dylan 2010

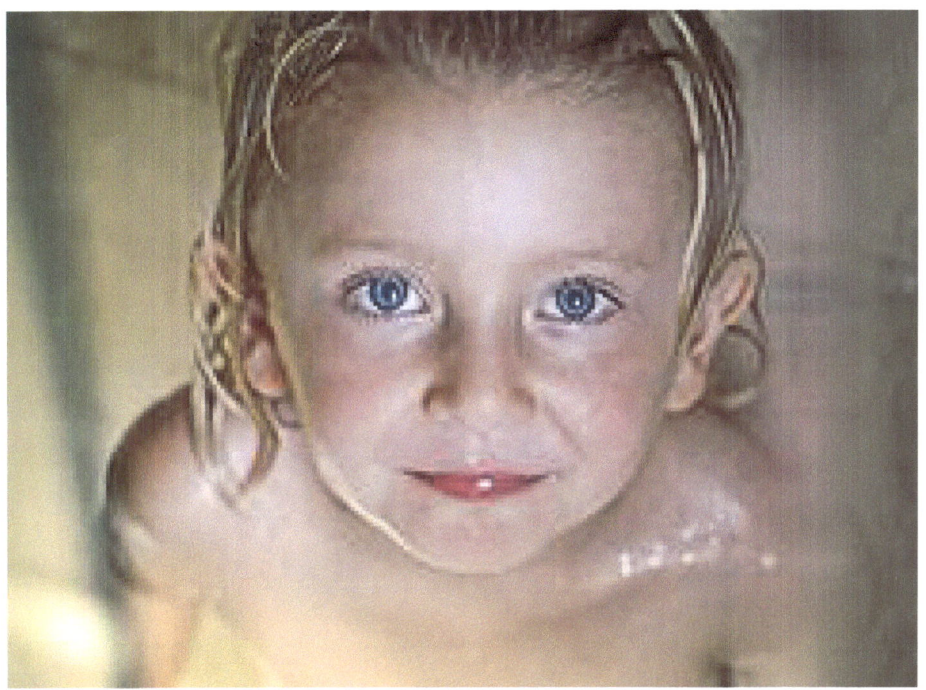

It's in their eyes... you can see the love in your child's eyes...
and you feel the love when their warm hand rests in yours... or they
grab your hear with "that smile. ... others see it, but only you know
"that smile"...

~ Sheryl Segal

Dylan 2010

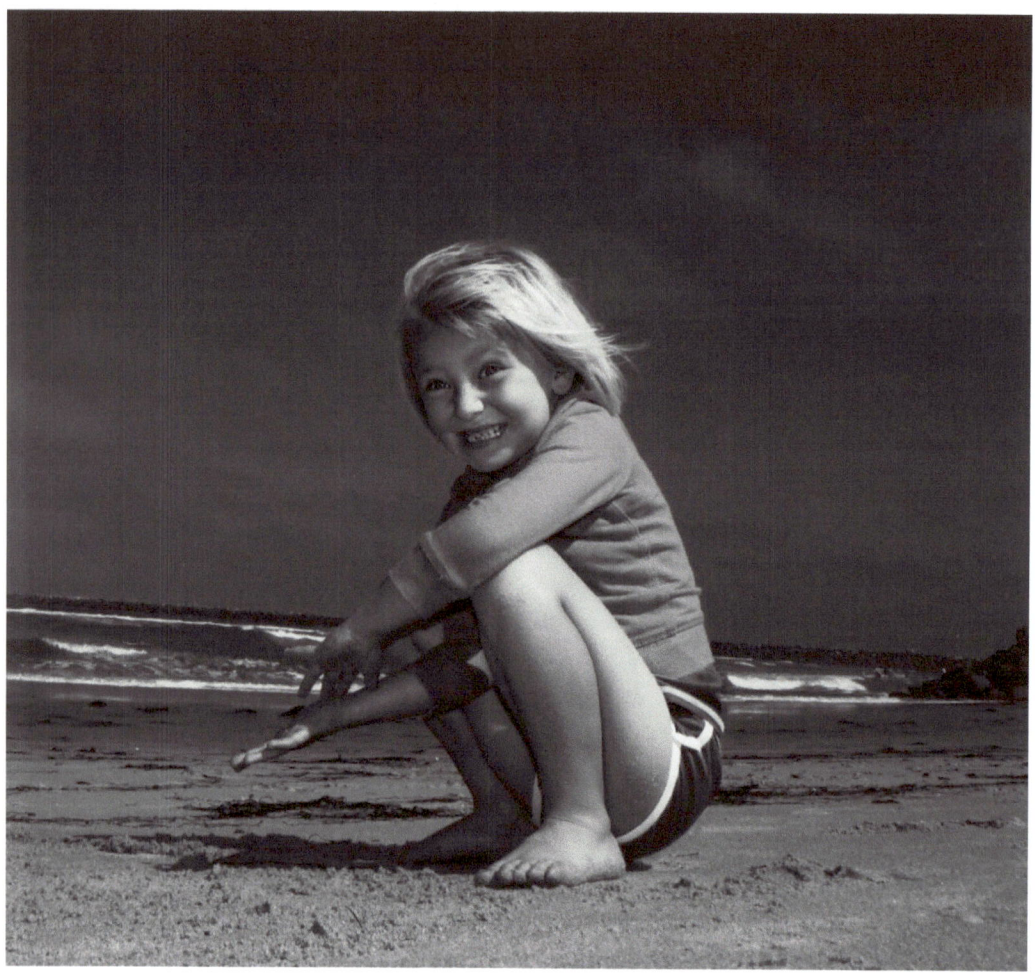

"I stay at Cindy and Brian's home often and there is a cool image in my room. One morning Dylan came in to give me a big welcome hug. I asked her about the simplistic image. I asked her if she did it, and she replied 'oh no, my daddy did, he's an amazing artist.' As I looked into her eyes full of love, respect and admiration for her father, I said 'yes precious girl, and you are one of his masterpieces!"

~ Kelly Hax

Dylan 2010

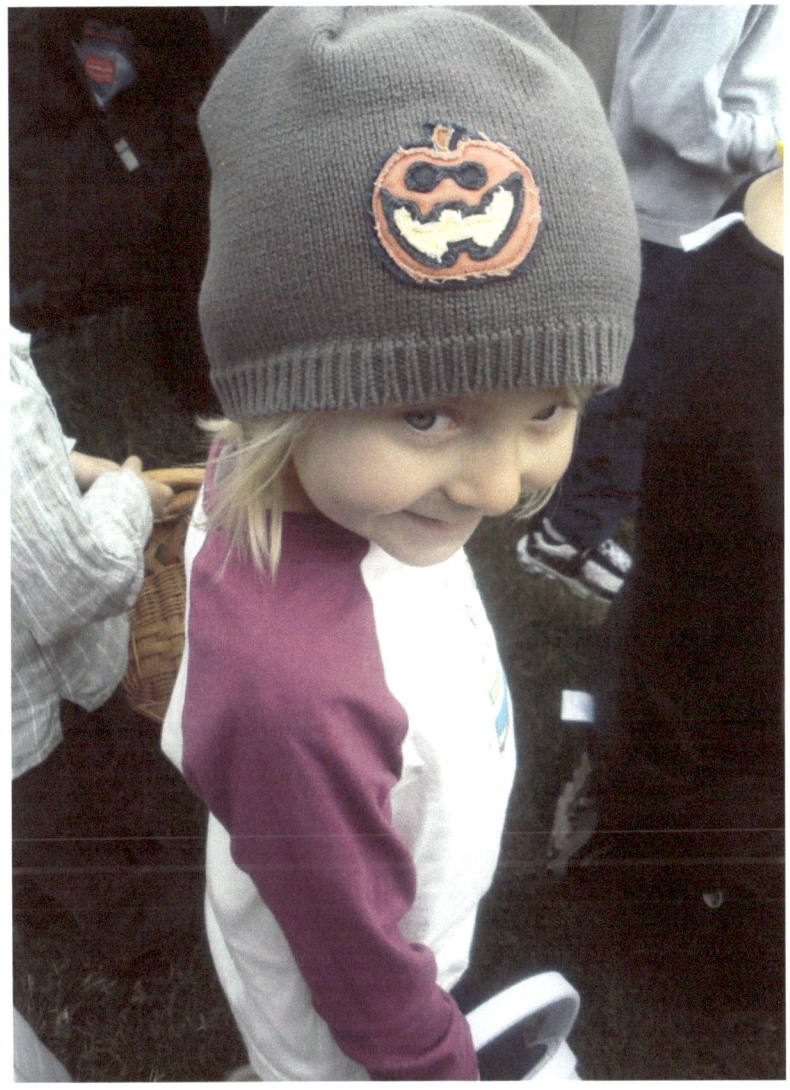

"Brian's photos of Dylan make Anne Geddes jealous. She is more technically skilled than he, but he has a much better model."

~ Mike Daugherty

Dylan 2005

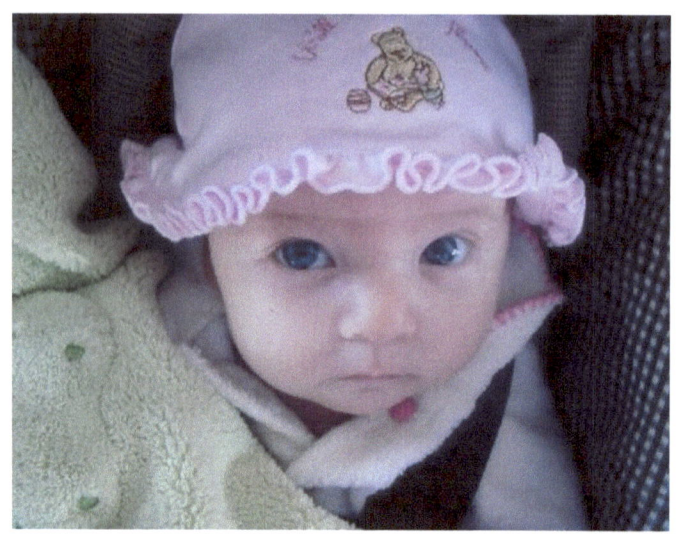

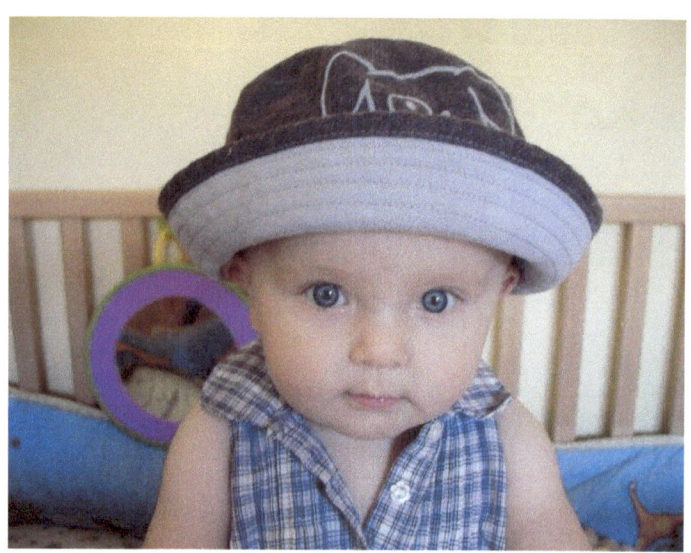

Dylan 2008

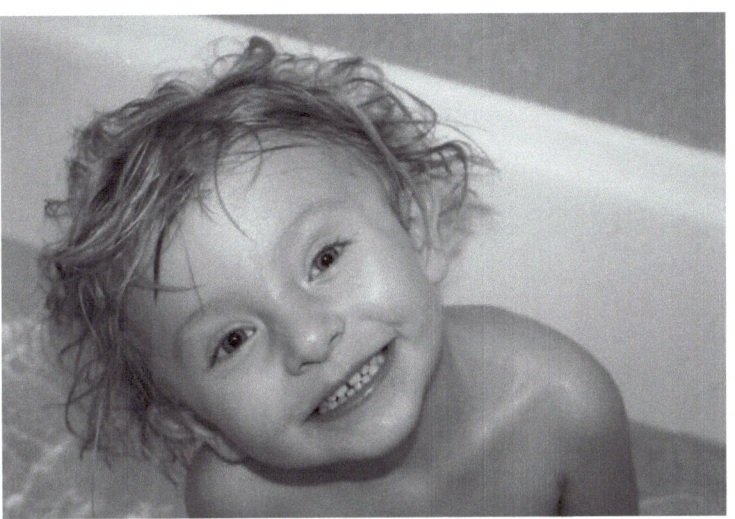

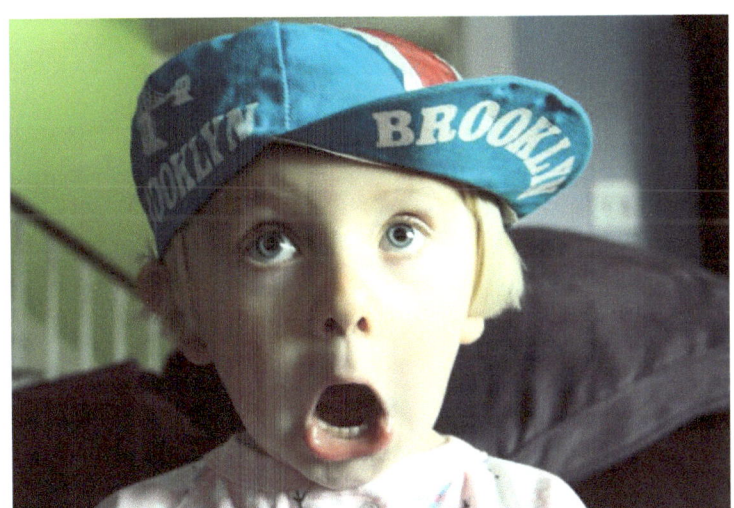

Dylan 2010

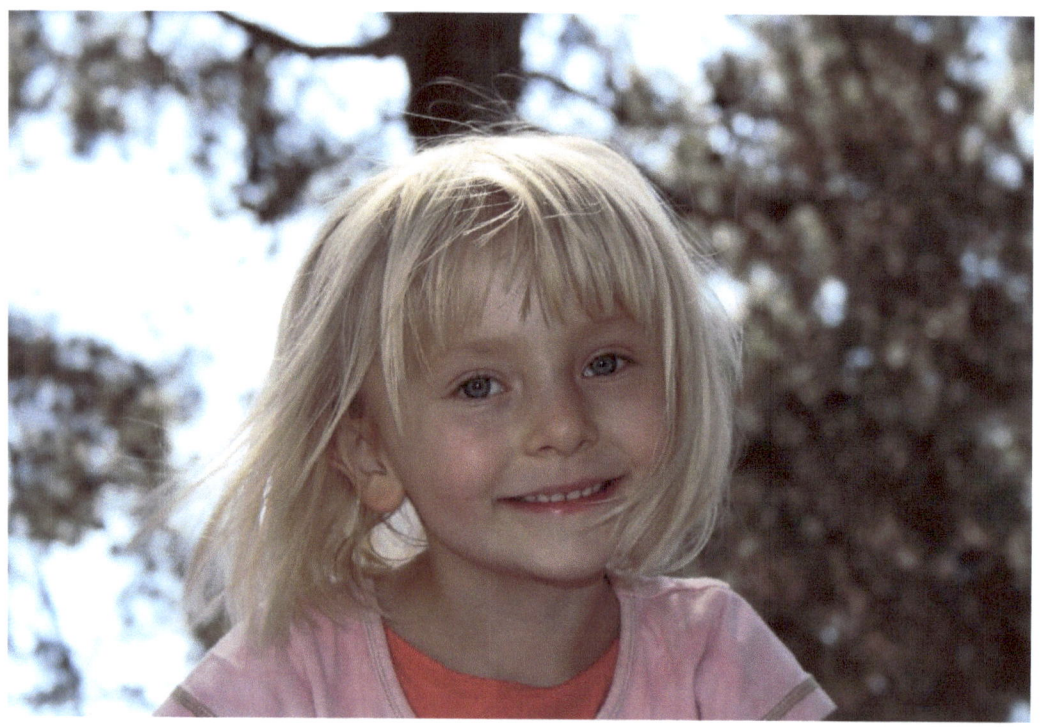

"The lens of a camera can capture only a small fraction of Dylan's radiant beauty and true personality, but it's worth trying. Brian does a great job capturing her."
~ Dave Larson

At Home Spa Compliments of Sophia ~ Dylan 2010

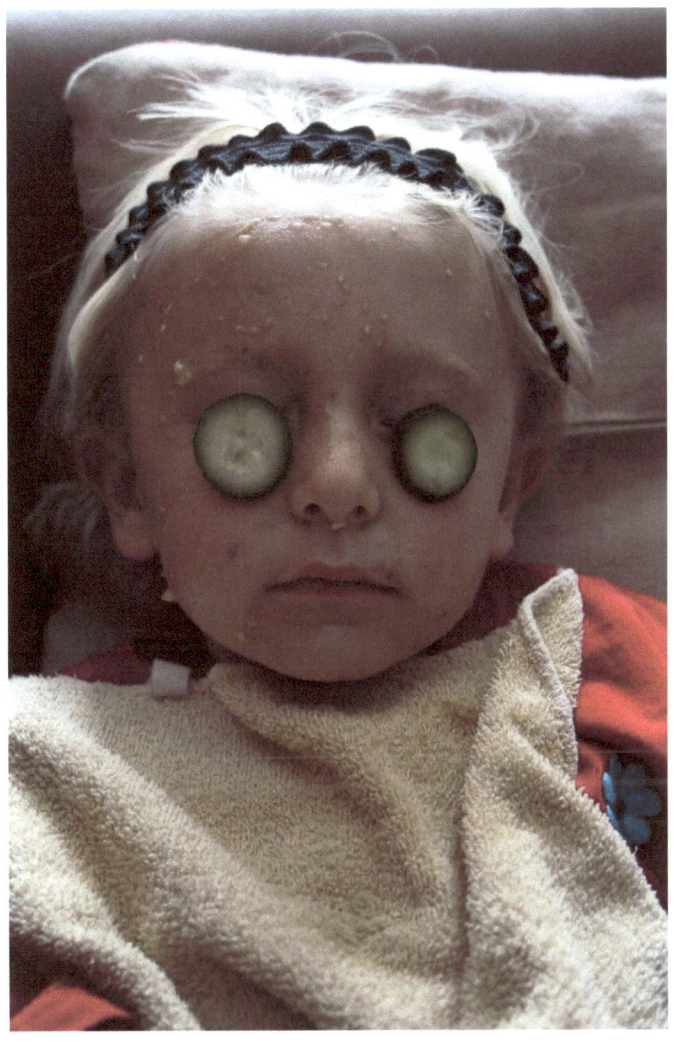

"Oh my God! I've been waiting for this all day. Pre-school was rough. I swear, if my teacher called on me one more time..." Dylan is utterly adorable and Brian seems to capture all her funny and beautiful moments.

~ Stacy Coombs Estolas

Dylan 2010

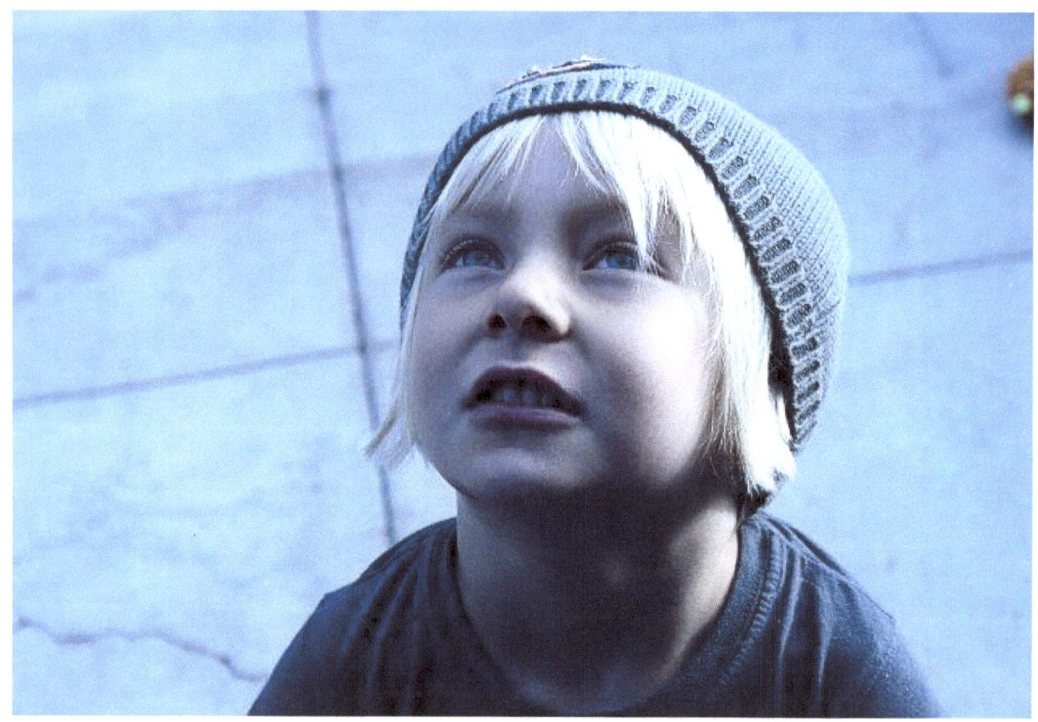

"One flew over the coo coos nest..Jack's character..that's the curious look I see in this photo. Dylan has many expressions and Brian seems to have a skill of capturing them at the right moment."

~ David Montes De Oca

Dylan 2010

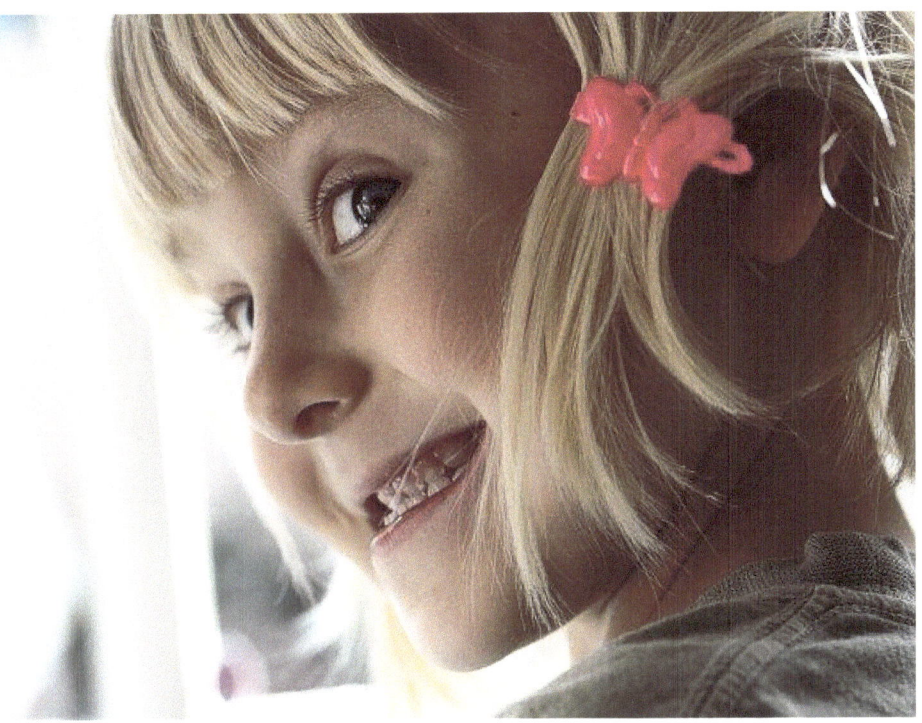

"Brian makes parenting look more fun and easy than anyone I have seen. She brings out a great side of him."

~ Steve H.

Dylan 2007

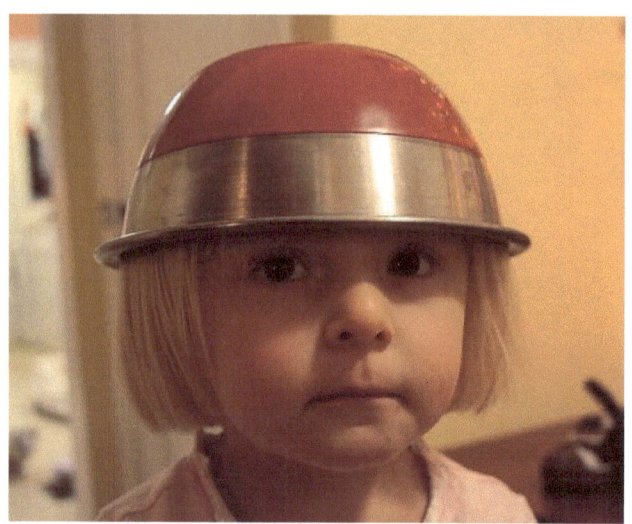

Dylan 2006

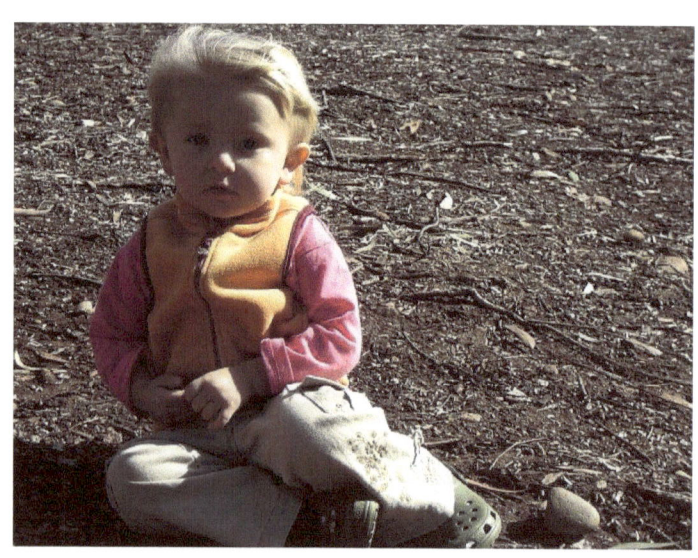

Dylan 2008

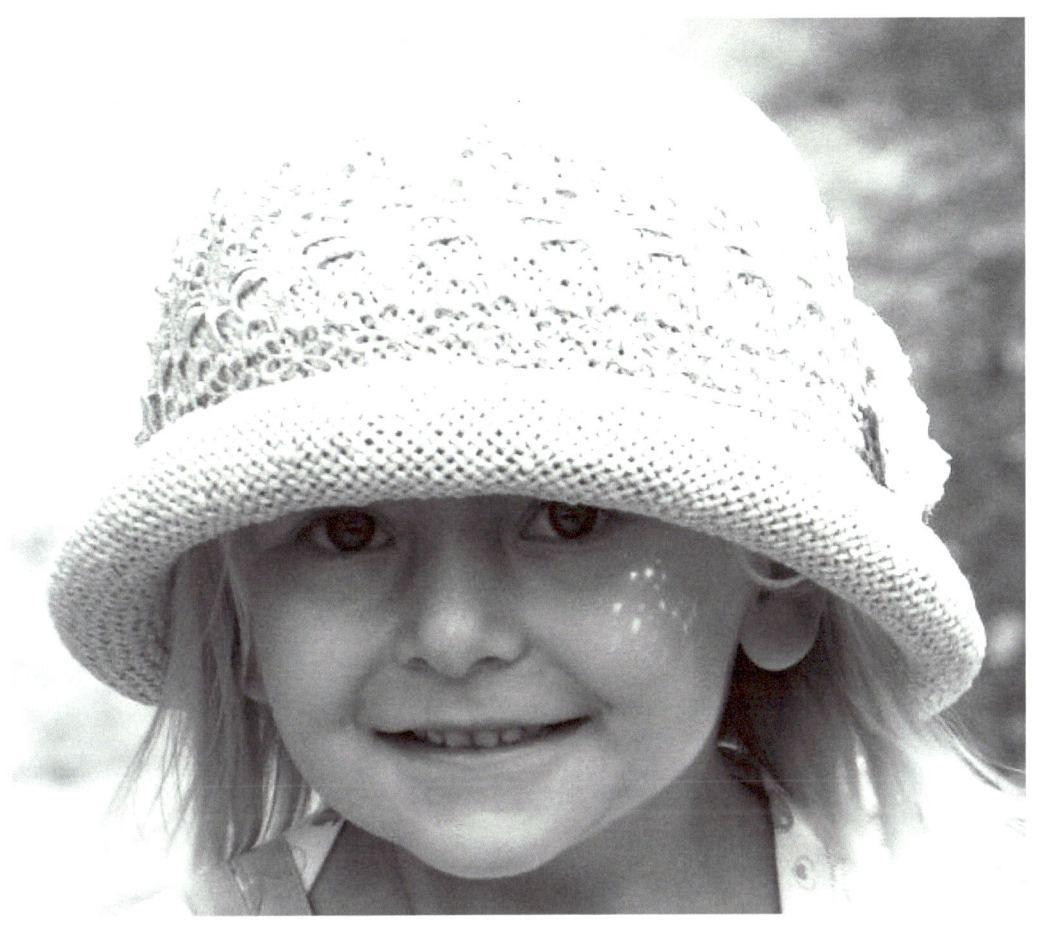

"This is one of my all time favorites as this is the little girl I see whether I am with her or just thinking about her."

~ Cindy

Dylan 2009

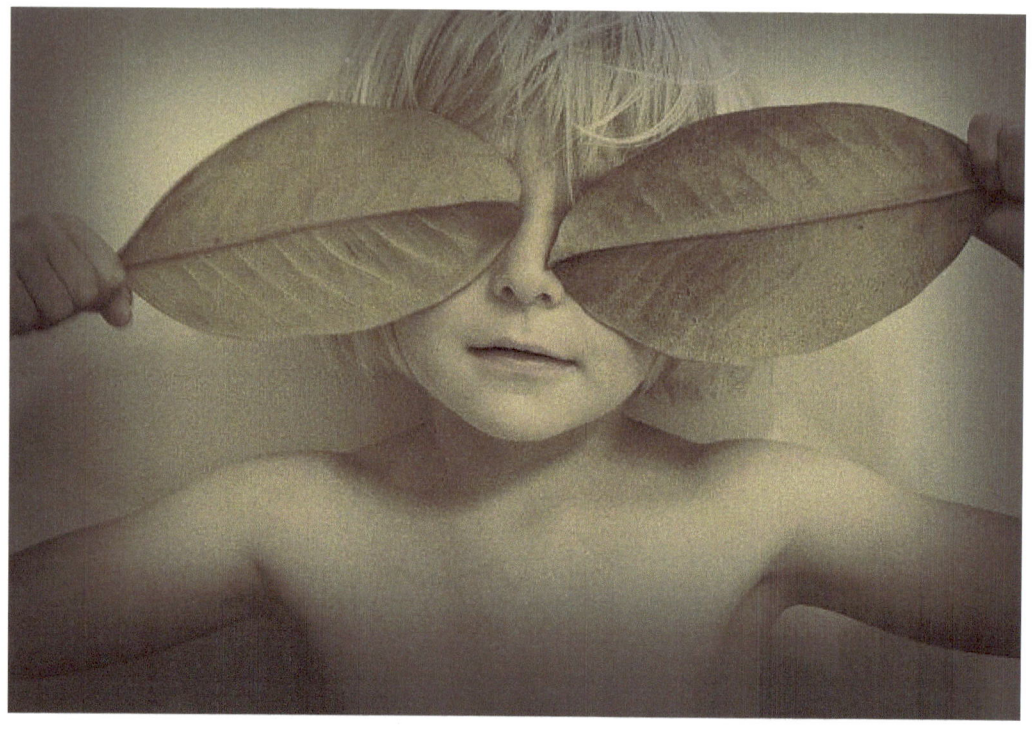

"Brian and I held a Nikon and Canon photo shoot context in the Grand Tetons and Yellow stone that ended in a tie. I don't think I could hold a candle to any of his Dylan photos. They are truly amazing."

~ Wendy Hershey

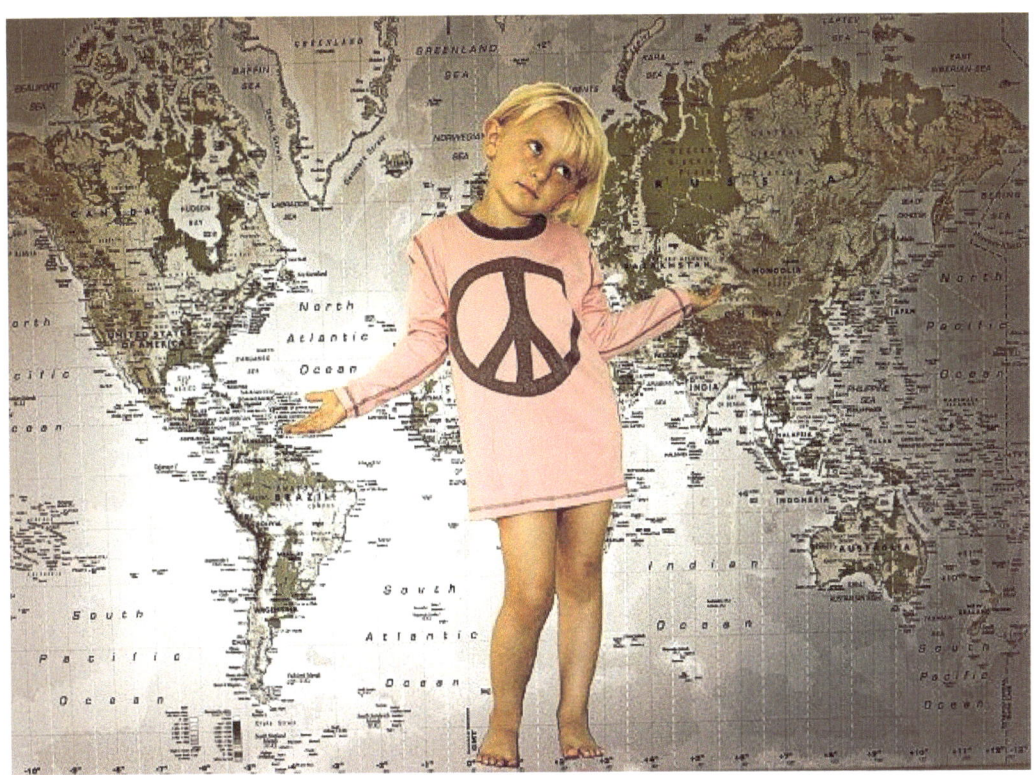

"From day one (maybe even before) I always knew 'Baby Daugherty' would be a beautiful genius. This amazing picture captures her inner and outer beauty, and she truly does wish for world peace..Grandma was right..she is a beautiful genius and Brian captures her perfectly."

~ Carol Larson

Dylan 2010

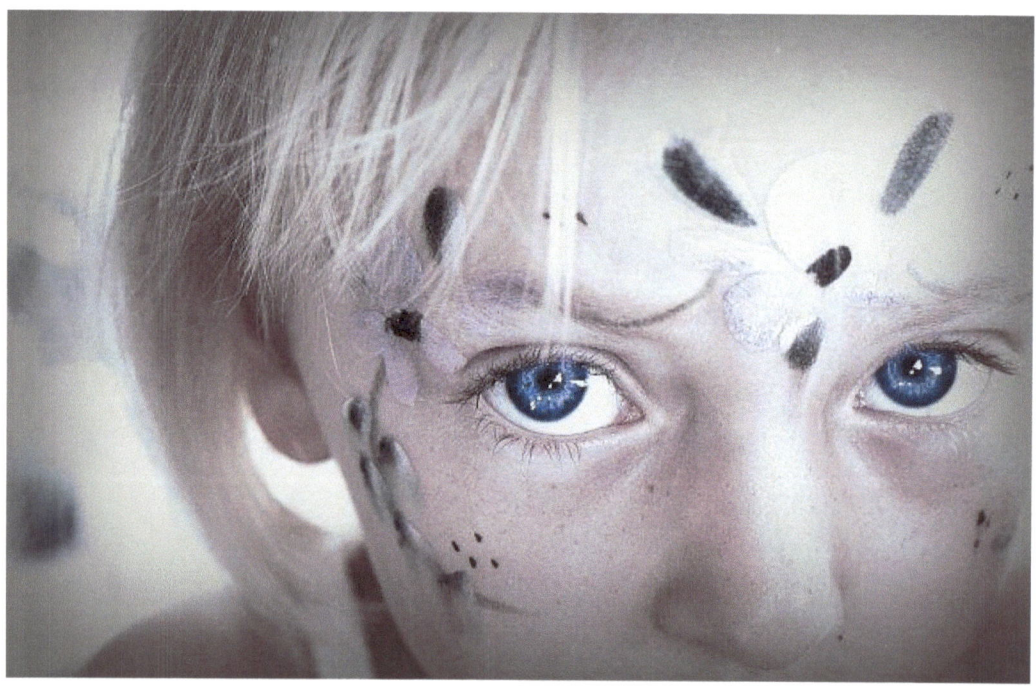

Brian's photography often reaches the level of poetry. Case in point, the pictures of Dylan, the daughter he adores, in all her many guises.

~ Greta Wheeler "The Nanny"

Dylan 2010

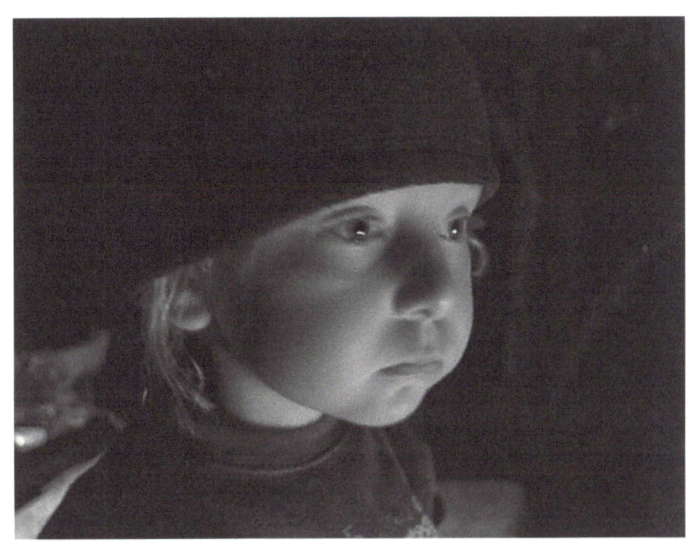

Dylan 2009

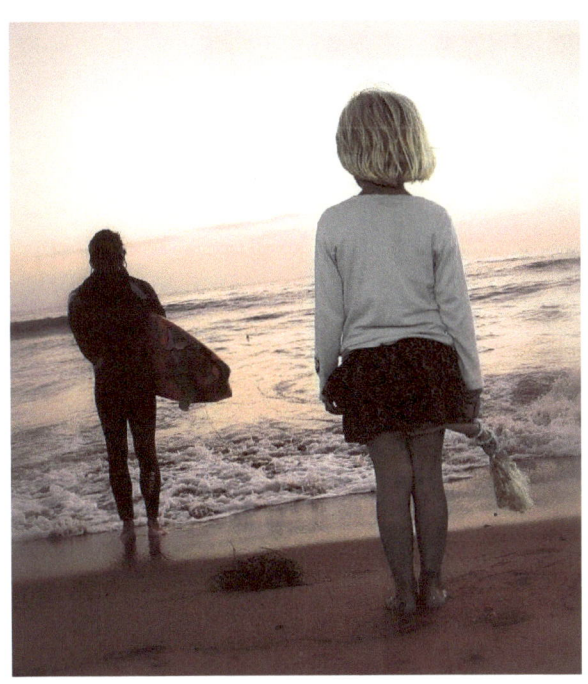

Dylan 2010

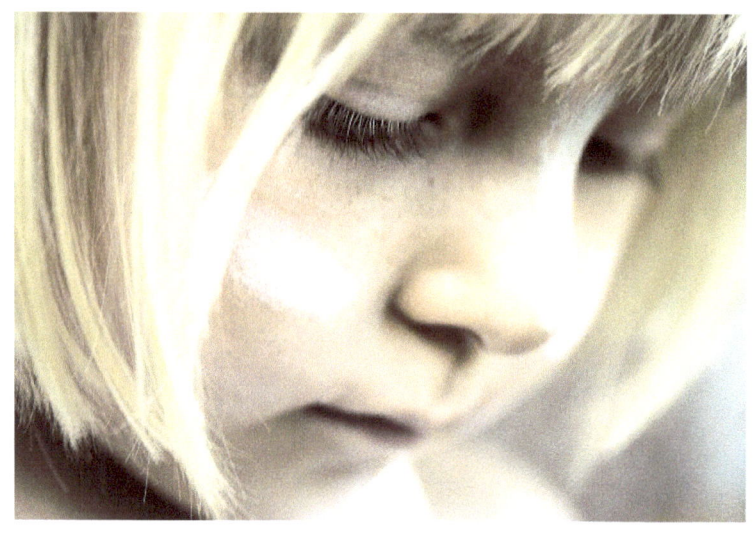

Dylan 2008

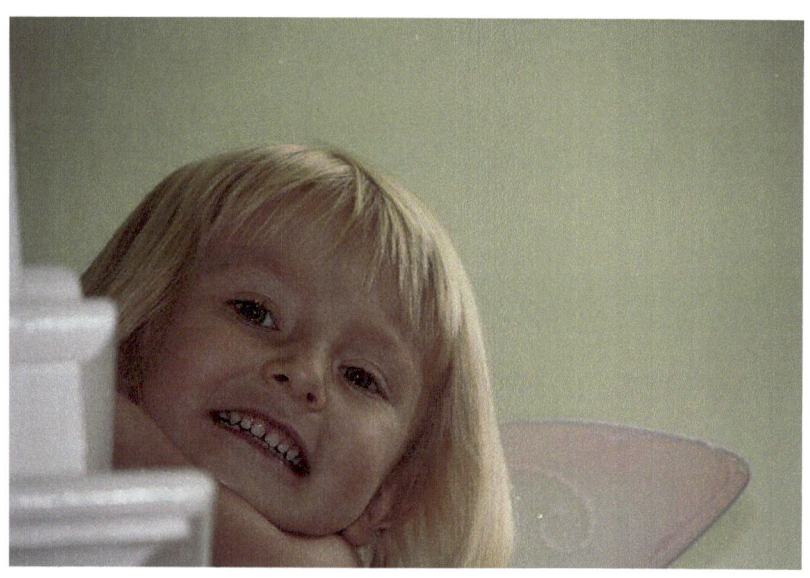

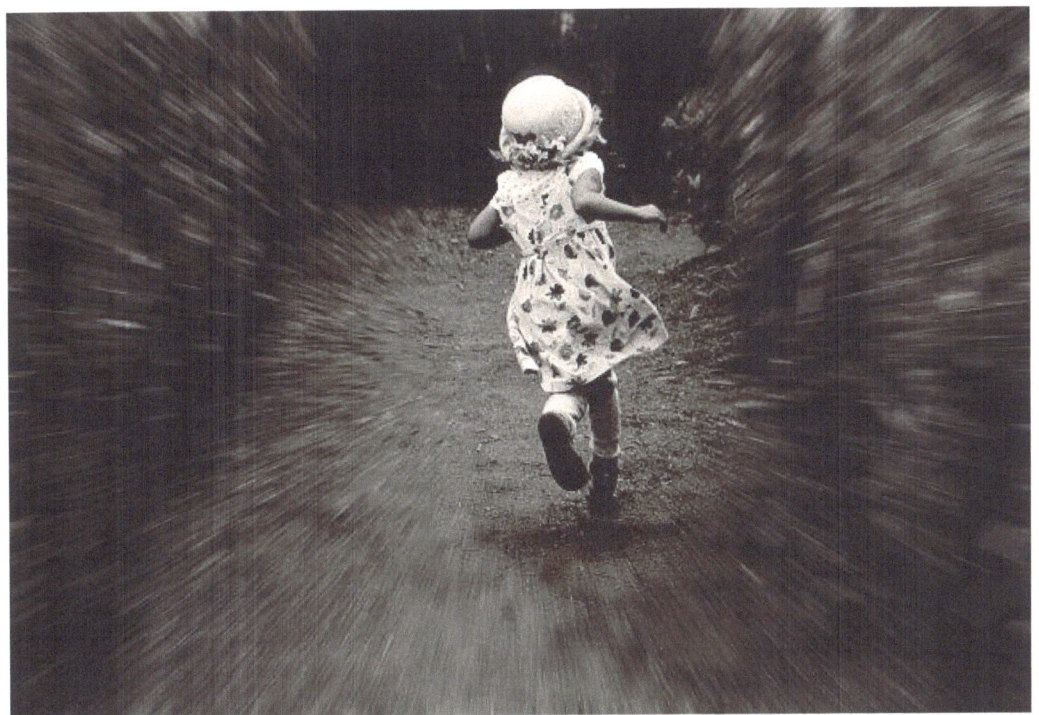

"Brian was starting to experiment with photography and things he could do with various software programs. I used to wonder why he spent all those hours on the computer, based on images like the one above, this journey of photographic love is all good with me."

~ Cindy

Ryan and Dylan 2010

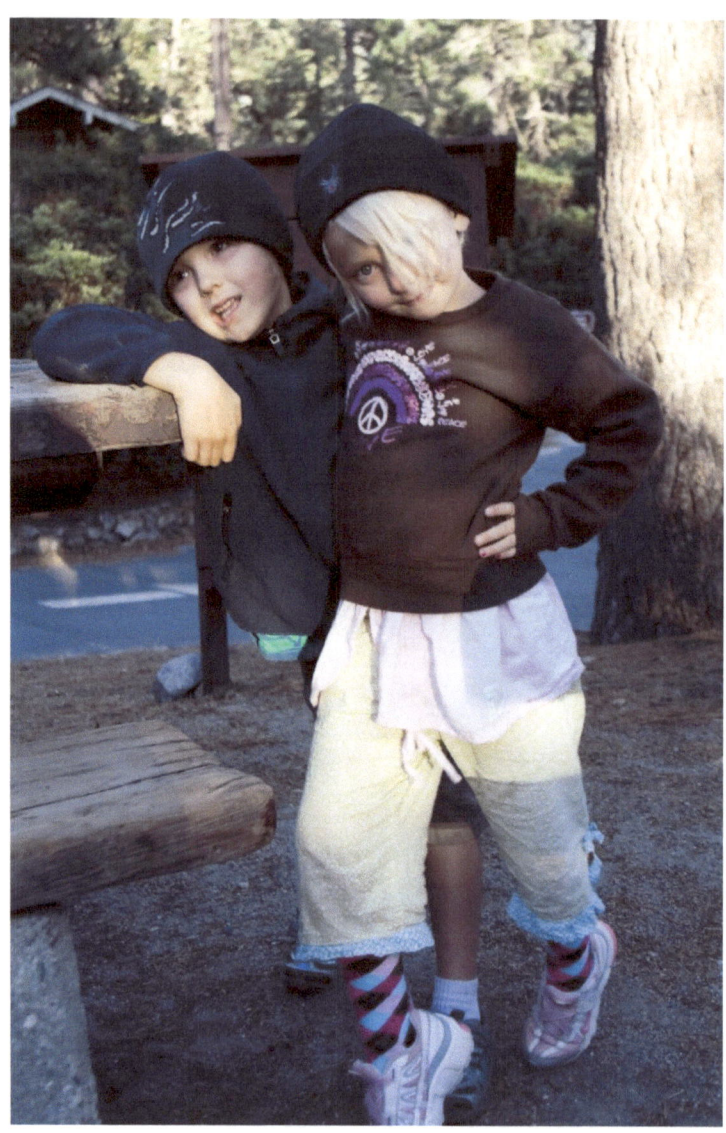

"I am with Ryan camping in this picture that Daddy took. I have known Ryan since we were babies. We might get married some day. I think it's okay with Daddy."

~ Dylan Mia

Part of Spring Soccer "Team Germany" –

Dylan, Carter behind her, Chopper, Max S., Max U. and Kenny 2010

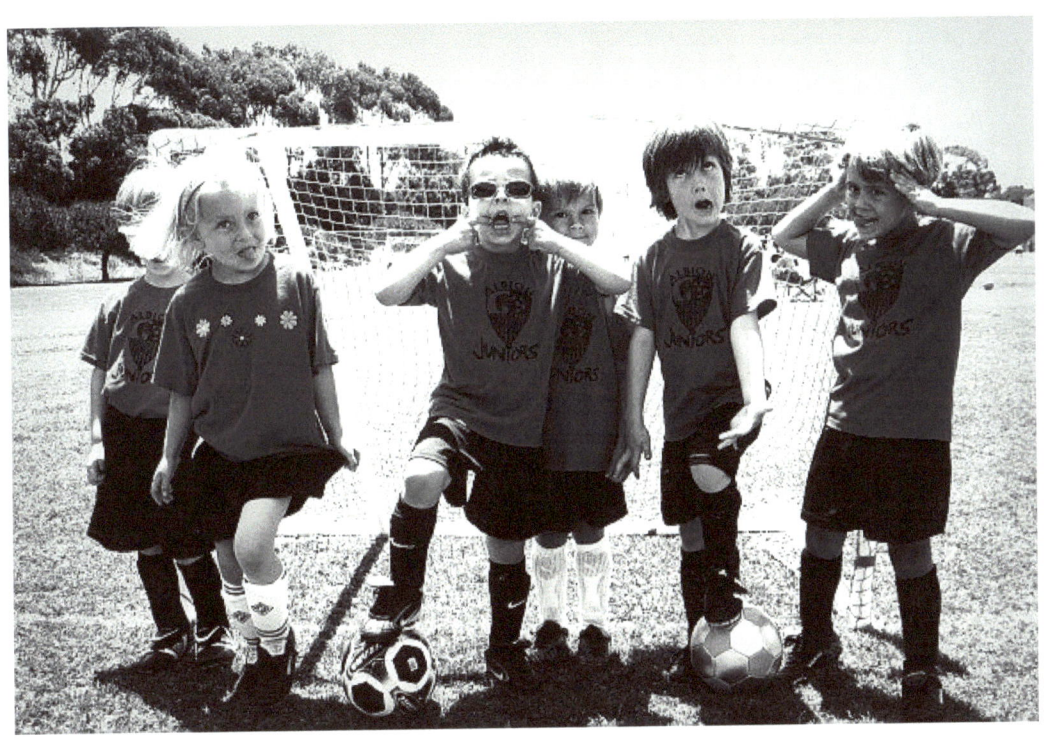

"Brian allowed these kids to be free and have fun. You can tell in their eyes that they love him and love being coached by him. I am torn on what I find most entertaining about this soccer season; watching the kids play or waiting for Brian's email review of the week. Thank you for yet another incredible year."

~ Paula Whalen (Kenny's Mom)

"Motivation is what gets you started. Coach Brian is what keeps you going."

~ Sandy Correia (Chopper's Mom)

Dylan and Cindy (mom) 2010

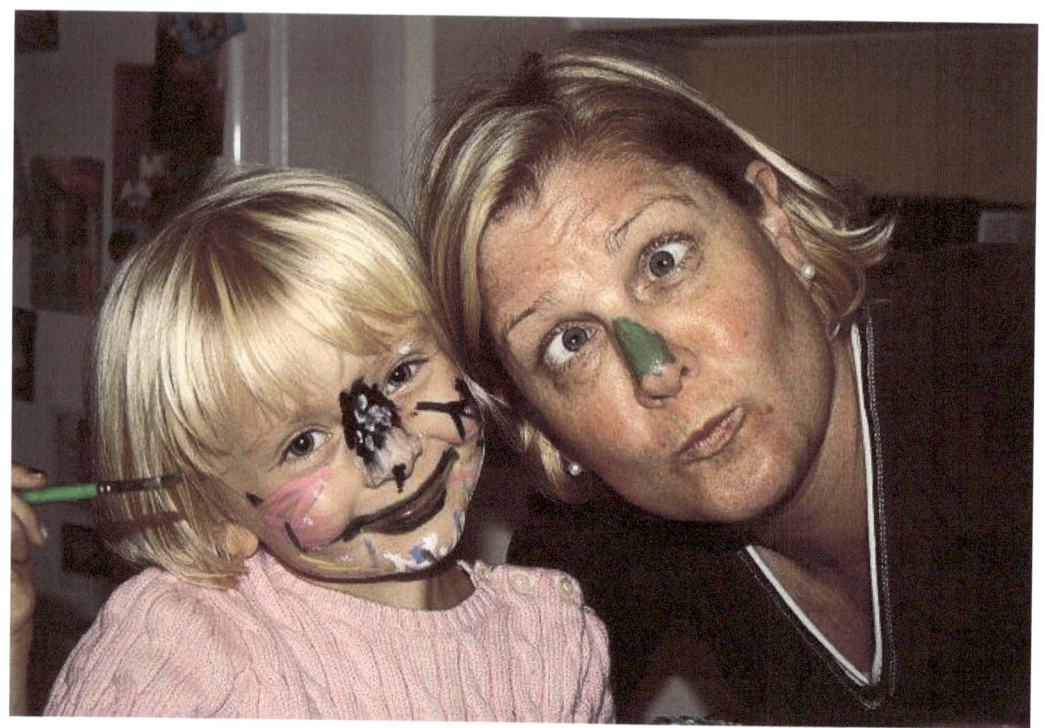

"I have learned three things in the past few years:
(1) being a parent you have to be pretty open to frequent silliness,
(2) Brian sees every moment as one to be captured no matter how silly the
subjects may look sometimes, and
(3) laughing at yourself is very good."
~ Cindy

Brian 2010

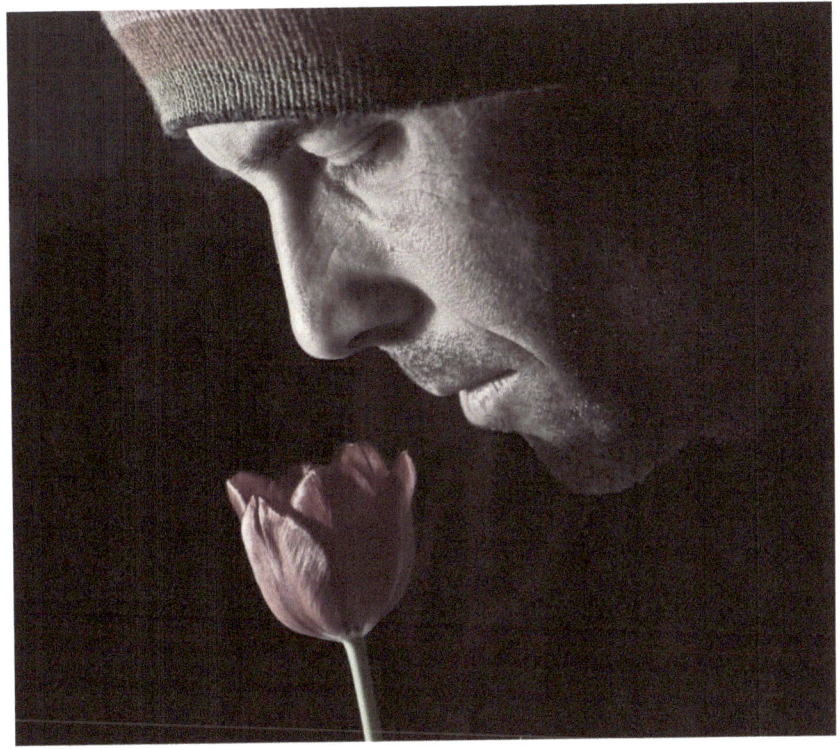

"When we were getting ready to publish this book Brian was on a trip and Dylan was really missing him. She said we needed to include a picture of Daddy. I asked her what this picture made her think and she said, "he looks serious, he must be thinking, maybe about me, well..maybe the flower too.."

~ Dylan Mia

Dylan and Brian 2010

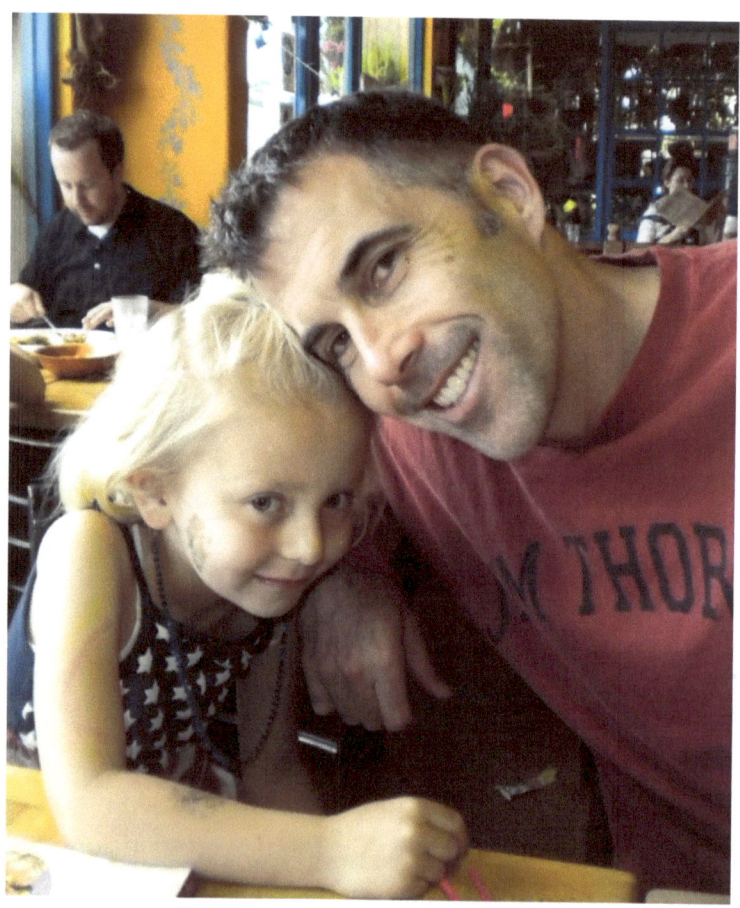

Brian and his favorite photographic subject Dylan
(the only photo not taken by Brian in the book)

Visit

www.agirlnameddylan.com

For more photos...

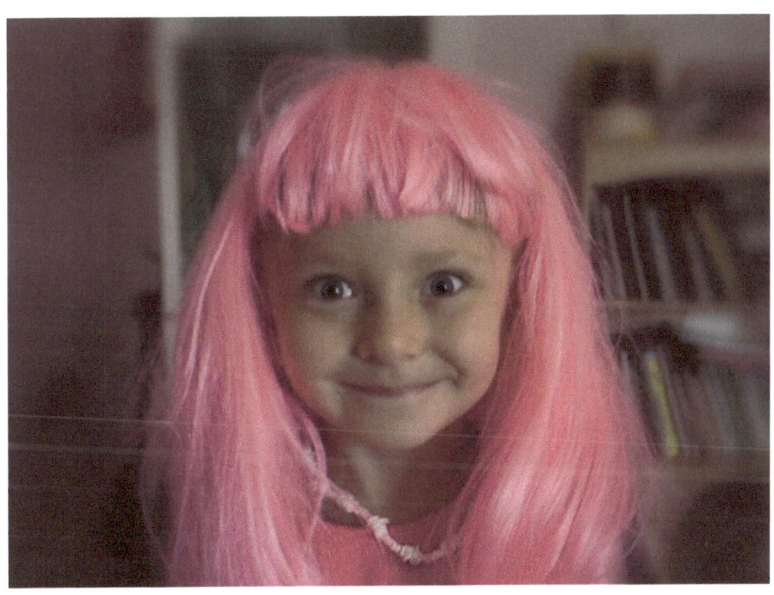

Thank you Felipe for sharing how you and Erica make it work so well after all these years ~ it's a great love story and reminded me it's always worth the effort. It inspired me to do something for Brian he's passionate about and would show him how much I love him.
Thank you Wendy for your help with picking photos and to all the other who provided thoughtful quotes.... Thank you....

www.ingramcontent.com/pod-product-compliance
Lightning Source LLC
Chambersburg PA
CBHW050403180526
45159CB00005B/2136